To Beatrice on the shower day
with lots of hugs & kisses

D1401959

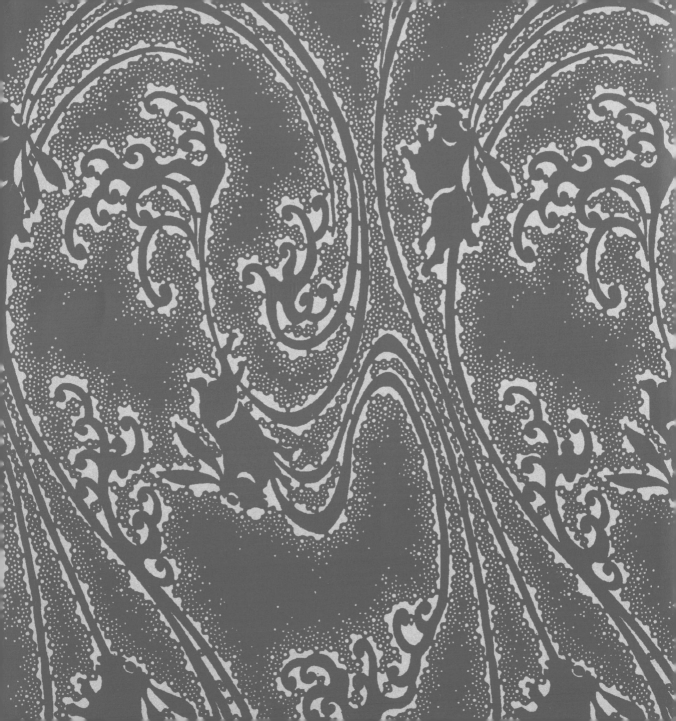

Married

IN THE MOVIES

EDITED BY KYLE RODERICK

CollinsPublishersSanFrancisco
A Division of HarperCollins*Publishers*

ACKNOWLEDGMENTS

The editor wishes to give special thanks to
Maura Carey Damacion, Linda Ferrer, and Sarah Bendersky
at Collins Publishers for their assistance on this book.
In addition, gratitude and kudos go to intrepid photo researchers
Peter Johnston, Andy Christie, and Marc Wanamaker of
Bison Archives, Los Angeles. Researcher Ernie Eban in London
provided valuable input. Kamal Kozah and Hugh McPherson
also provided valuable research help.
Thanks again to the top-notch staff at the Academy of Motion
Picture Arts and Sciences' Margaret Herrick Library.

First published 1994
by Collins Publishers San Francisco
1160 Battery Street
San Francisco, California 94111

Designed by Jacqueline Jones Design, San Francisco

Library of Congress Cataloging in Publication Data
Married in the Movies.
1. Weddings in motion pictures--Pictorial works.
I. Roderick, Kyle.
PN1995.9M3M37 1994 791.43'654 93-34291
ISBN 0-00-255368-6

Printed in Italy
10 9 8 7 6 5 4 3 2 1

"Marriage is a great institution," Mae West once said,

"But I'm not ready for an institution."

Hollywood was. Right from the start, the earliest one and two

reelers featured weddings. In fact, it was hard to keep some moviemakers

away from orange blossoms and white lace. Maybe it was the built-in

excuse for extravagant costumes. Or maybe it was the inherent drama of

weddings, or the fact that everyone knew the lines. From a director's

point of view, whether weddings made a satisfactory windup, a perfect

romantic interlude, or a melodramatic mismatch, they ended in

that surefire clinch.

As early as 1911, Thomas Edison produced *The Wedding Bell,*

an attack on the evils of tenement life that climaxed with the bride collapsing from typhoid. By the 1920s, the movies had graduated to

more sophisticated scenarios, but weddings still scored at the box office.

As the decades progressed, weddings on-screen veered from elaborate

to refreshingly realistic to downright surreal.

    This book spans seven decades of movie matrimony. While far

from a comprehensive wedding album, it'll get you to the church on time

to see Sophia Loren marry Cary Grant, Marlon Brando give away

Talia Shire, and Ali MacGraw and Ryan O'Neal embark on their smash

box office *Love Story*. Of course, we don't guarantee happy endings.

That only happens in the movies.

THE GAY BRIDE

"Small" and "intimate" didn't
spell big box office in
Hollywood during
the Depression. Even in a
routine programmer like this,
the studios pulled
out the stops. Here Carole
Lombard and Nat Pendleton
tie the knot amid more
bridesmaids, blossoms, and
swings (!) than you can shake
a stick at.

1934

EASY TO WED

Decisions, decisions. Van Johnson is torn between a pre-bathing suited Esther Williams (left) and a pre-"I Love Lucy" Lucille Ball (right). This remake of the 1930s screwball comedy *Libeled Lady* featured Williams as a society girl and Ball as a tough-talking honey, with Johnson as a reporter caught between the two.

1946

THE LADY EVE

With its seven-foot, cathedral-length train and four layers of net in the veil, this satin sheath, designed by Edith Head, epitomizes old-fashioned Hollywood glamour. About to get hitched to millionaire scientist Henry Fonda, Barbara Stanwyck looks to the manor born as the title character in Preston Sturges' classic comedy.

1941

EVERYBODY'S ALL-AMERICAN

Beautiful cheerleader Jessica Lange takes her football hero husband
Dennis Quaid for better and for worse in this gridiron soap opera. Lange
ages in the movie from a teenager to a middle-aged mom.

1988

THE SOUND OF MUSIC

How do you solve a problem like Maria? The nuns think they have found the answer as they escort Julie Andrews to the altar. Based on the memoirs of Maria von Trapp, who fled the Nazis with her family in 1938, this blockbuster musical featured Rodgers and Hammerstein's beloved score.

1965

FATHER
OF THE BRIDE

Vincente Minnelli directed
this classic look at the rituals
surrounding a plush subur-
ban wedding, with Dad
(Spencer Tracy) taking it all
harder than everyone else.
Elizabeth Taylor is the
improbably beautiful bride
of the title. Within days
of the movie's opening, ver-
sions of her dress appeared
in department stores across
the country.

1950

FATHER OF THE BRIDE

Steve Martin stepped into Tracy's role in the remake, giving away daughter Kimberly
Williams in the midst of major mid-life angst. By the time this remake hit the screen,
weddings no longer were make-or-break events which determined a family's community
status, so the focus shifted to the internal problems of Martin's character.

1991

ABIE'S IRISH ROSE

The movie version of
the long-running Broadway
comedy about a Jewish
boy (Buddy Rogers), who
secretly marries an Irish girl
(Nancy Carroll), and then
tries to placate both sets
of in-laws, featured titles by
Herman J. Mankiewicz
and a priest and a rabbi on the
set as technical advisors.

1928

HAIR

The Age of Aquarius? John Savage's LSD-induced
hallucinations include Beverly D'Angelo as a pregnant bride
floating above Hare Krishna-chanting bridesmaids. Milos
Forman directed this exuberant movie version.

1979

**MARRIAGE IS A PRIVATE
AFFAIR**

And man-chasing Lana
Turner is determined to keep
it that way despite the
ring on her finger after she
marries James Craig.

1944

CAMELOT

Despite a budget
of $15 million, this lush
version of Lerner and Lowe's
Broadway musical didn't take
off at the box office. Still,
it's hard to fault the casting
of the ethereally lovely
Vanessa Redgrave as
Guenevere or the virile and
versatile Richard Harris
as Arthur.

1967

THE PHILADELPHIA STORY

Heading down the aisle a second time, Philadelphia socialite
Katharine Hepburn finds herself back where she started with husband
number one (Cary Grant). Jimmy Stewart is the reporter she nearly
falls for along the way in Philip Barry's witty comedy.

1940

HIGH SOCIETY

In her last role before
accepting a real-life crown,
society princess Grace
Kelly remarries ex-hubby
Bing Crosby in this
Philadelphia Story remake.

1956

THE GRADUATE

Dustin Hoffman arrives too late to prevent ex-girlfriend Katharine Ross's
wedding, but just in time to break up her marriage. She flees the church with him to the fading
strains of Simon and Garfunkel's memorable score. Mike Nichols won an Academy
award for best direction.

1967

FUNNY FACE

S'wonderful, s'marvelous,
s'Fred Astaire and Audrey
Hepburn and the gown's
by Givenchy.

1957

THE BRIDE WORE CRUTCHES

Lynne Roberts proves you can't keep a good woman down in this
little-known comedy when she refuses to let a leg injury halt her nuptials.
Robert Armstrong is the groom who hoists her to the altar.

1941

THE BRIDE WORE BOOTS

A horse is a horse, of course, but this unusual wedding party includes the
hoofer who reunites gorgeous equestrienne Barbara Stanwyck with her literary
ex-husband, Robert Cummings. Peggy Wood and Robert Benchley look on.

1946

THE OLD MAID

Based on an Edith Wharton novel, this weepie has Bette Davis,
gorgeously gowned by Orry-Kelly, forced to abandon her wedding plans
at the last moment for fear of exposing her illegitimate child.

1939

CHILDREN OF DIVORCE

Esther Ralston's lacy
gown has the sleek flapper
silhouette of the day.

1927

THE FAMILY WAY

Judging from their expressions, Hayley Mills and Hywel Bennett
have a premonition married life won't be a bed of roses. With a score by Paul
McCartney, this British comedy looks at the travails of a newlywed couple.

1966

THE GIRL WHO COULDN'T SAY NO

George Segal and Virna Lisi tie the knot, then have a hard time keeping
it that way in this Italian-made comedy.

1969

WAIKIKI WEDDING

The hulas and the orchids
nearly eclipse Shirley
Ross in Hollywood's goofy
salute to an improbably
exotic Hawaii. Bing Crosby
also starred.

1937

GENTLEMEN PREFER BLONDES

Under Howard Hawks' capable direction, the two little girls
from Little Rock make their way down the aisle. Marilyn Monroe is sultry
gold digger Lorelei Lee and Jane Russell is her good-natured sidekick.

1953

OUR MODERN MAIDENS (LEFT)
THE TAMING OF THE SHREW (BELOW)

A young Joan Crawford and even younger Douglas Fairbanks, Jr.
became one of Tinseltown's golden couples when they tied the knot in real life.
Still, they posed no threat to then-reigning legends (and Dad and Stepmom)
Douglas Fairbanks, Sr. and Mary Pickford, seen here in their only
on-screen appearance together.

1929

THE HEARTBREAK KID

Elaine May directs
daughter, and bride, Jeannie
Berlin in this comedy
about a nice Jewish boy
(Charles Grodin) who meets
the ultimate *shiksa* (Cybill
Shepherd) on his honeymoon,
with tragicomic results.

1972

BEETLEJUICE

Director Tim Burton's macabre comedy has Michael Keaton as the
ghostly title character nearly nabbing Winona Ryder. Her presence of mind saves
her at the last minute and sends Beetlejuice back to his otherworldly haunts.
Understandably, this film won an Academy award for best makeup.

1988

COVER GIRL

Rita Hayworth has a faraway look in her eye that spells trouble for
groom Lee Bowman in this musical. She's about to make a run for Brooklyn
and the waiting arms of Gene Kelly.

1944

PROFESSOR BEWARE

Comedian Harold
Lloyd is the groom captured
—so to speak—in the
lens of director Elliott
Nugent's camera. In this
rare on-the-set still, his bride
is Phyllis Welch.

1938

GOODBYE, COLUMBUS

Ali MacGraw and Richard Benjamin are Phillip Roth's unhappy young lovers,
hanging out here with Jack Klugman at a lavish wedding reception.

1969

LOVE STORY

Love means never having
to say you're sorry for Ryan O'Neal
as a wealthy WASP and Ali MacGraw
as his wrong-side-of-the-tracks
beloved. Almost before their marriage
gets off the ground, MacGraw develops
a convenient terminal illness.

1970

THE QUIET MAN

Director John Ford brought his cast and crew to Ireland to shoot
this story of an Irish-American boxer who retires to the Emerald Isle and wins
the love of colleen Maureen O'Hara. Abbey Theatre School graduate
O'Hara gets a speech in Gaelic, as well as a traditional lace-and-linen gown
to offset those sensible shoes.

1952

HELLO, DOLLY!

One look at the cast of hundreds and Irene Sharaff's costumes and you can see where the movie's then-staggering $24 million budget went. Director Gene Kelly pulled out all the stops for matchmaker Dolly Levi's (Barbra Streisand) wedding to wealthy grain merchant Horace Vandergelder (Walter Matthau).

1969

OKLAHOMA!

The corn is as high as an elephant's eye when Curly (Gordon MacRae)
and Laurey (Shirley Jones) finally get hitched in this version of Rodgers and
Hammerstein's groundbreaking musical.

1955

TAHITI NIGHTS

Unlikely islander Clyde Fillmore joins David O'Brien and Mary Treen
in South Pacific-style matrimony.

1945

THE PALM BEACH STORY

Claudette Colbert and Joel McCrea marry in haste and repent quite a bit in this
screwball comedy by Preston Sturges.

1942

I WAS A MALE WAR BRIDE

Cary Grant sports a fetching skirt and wig in nearly every scene following
his wedding to "Oomph" girl Ann Sheridan. As a French army officer trying to
accompany his WAC wife back to the United States, Grant spends
much of the movie in drag.

1949

HOUSEBOAT

A summer aboard with Sophia
Loren as housekeeper *(mama mia!)*
convinces widower Cary Grant that
it's time to take another plunge.
His kids reluctantly agree that a new
mom means a new wife for Dad.

1958

THE BRIDE
OF FRANKENSTEIN

You can't blame Elsa
Lanchester for her reaction
as she recoils in horror at
her first sight of monster-
groom Boris Karloff in this
horror camp classic.

1935

GONE WITH THE WIND

Not one to stand by
tamely while the love of her
life Ashley Wilkes (Leslie
Howard) plights his troth to
another woman (Olivia
de Havilland), Vivien Leigh's
Scarlett O'Hara wastes
no time in marching down
the aisle herself. Any
hopes of teaching Ashley a
lesson are dashed at the
reception when he has eyes
only for his wife.

1939

A WEDDING

As the lovelorn mother-of-the-bride, Carol Burnett nearly steals the
show in Robert Altman's affectionate satire of a nouveau riche wedding. Paul
Dooley, Mia Farrow, Dennis Christopher, and Amy Stryker (as the
lackluster bride) make up her oblivious family.

1978

SERIAL

New Age meets a Smothers
brother as Martin Mull and
Tuesday Weld renew their
vows in an ultrasolemn ceremony led by Reverend Spike
(Tommy Smothers).

1980

THE DEMI-BRIDE

Here Reverend Neal Dodd, a popular Tinseltown clergyman who married
scores of actors both in real life and on screen, unites Norma Shearer and Lew
Cody. The cake she cuts looks to be about an acre across. Shearer, who
in real life was the fortunate bride of boy-wonder producer Irving Thalberg,
went on to a successful career in talking pictures.

1927

PRIVATE BENJAMIN

Goldie Hawn's wedding night has an unexpected climax when her
husband (Albert Brooks) dies of a heart attack. Uncle Sam provides plenty
of distractions when she joins the army to get over her grief.

1980

I LOVE YOU, ALICE B. TOKLAS!

Despite the yarmulke, Peter Sellers won't be standing under the canopy.
In this 1960s counterculture celebration, he plays a nebbishy lawyer who ditches
Jo van Fleet at the altar—not once but twice.

1968

STORMY WEATHER

Twentieth Century Fox's
wartime roundup
of Hollywood's African-
American talent features
Lena Horne and Bill
"Bojangles" Robinson in
a wispy romance that finally
sees them united.

1943

BROKEN ARROW

With Hollywood leery of seeming to endorse miscegenation, it's no
surprise that Debra Paget's Native-American princess bride bites the dust
before the honeymoon with groom Jimmy Stewart is over.

1950

DANCES WITH WOLVES

Politically correct Civil War vet Kevin Costner marries
Stands-with-a-Fist, a.k.a. Mary McDonnell, in a traditional Lakota
Sioux ceremony. Interestingly, both are Caucasian, suggesting that Hollywood
still hasn't gotten comfortable with interracial marriage, forty
years after *Broken Arrow*. The historically accurate costumes were
designed by Elsa Zamparelli.

1990

THE GODFATHER

Francis Ford Coppola's epic tale of a Mafia dynasty features one of
Hollywood's most famous weddings. *Capo di tutti capi* Don Corleone (Marlon
Brando) gives away daughter Gina (Talia Shire) in a lavish ceremony
that set a new Italian-American standard. Al Pacino, John Cazale, and James
Caan—who seduces a bridesmaid in passing—are his other children.

1972

FIDDLER ON THE ROOF

Tradition, tradition! Leonard Frey and Rosalind Harris
happily break it at their wedding celebration in this big-screen
version of the Broadway musical.

1971

FLOWER DRUM SONG

Rodgers and Hammerstein scored another hit with this musical. The
screen adaptation features a double wedding with traditional bride Miyoshi
Umeki wearing a gold-ribboned veil and flowered headdress and modern
bride Nancy Kwan wearing a mandarin-collared gown, with gloves
and spike heels. Costumes are by Irene Sharaff.

1961

GUYS AND DOLLS

Miss Adelaide (Vivian Blaine) finally gets her man
(Frank Sinatra) in the MGM version of the Jo Swerling-
Abe Burrows-Frank Loesser Broadway hit.

1955

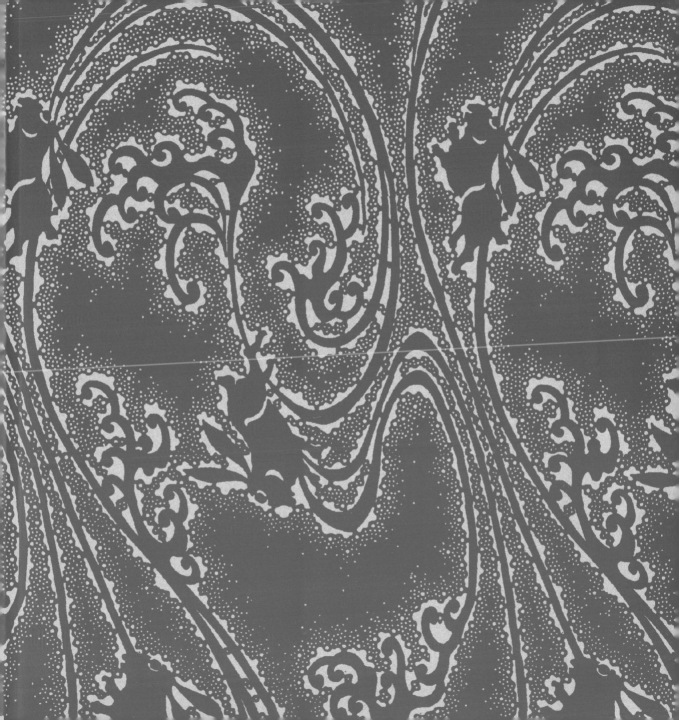

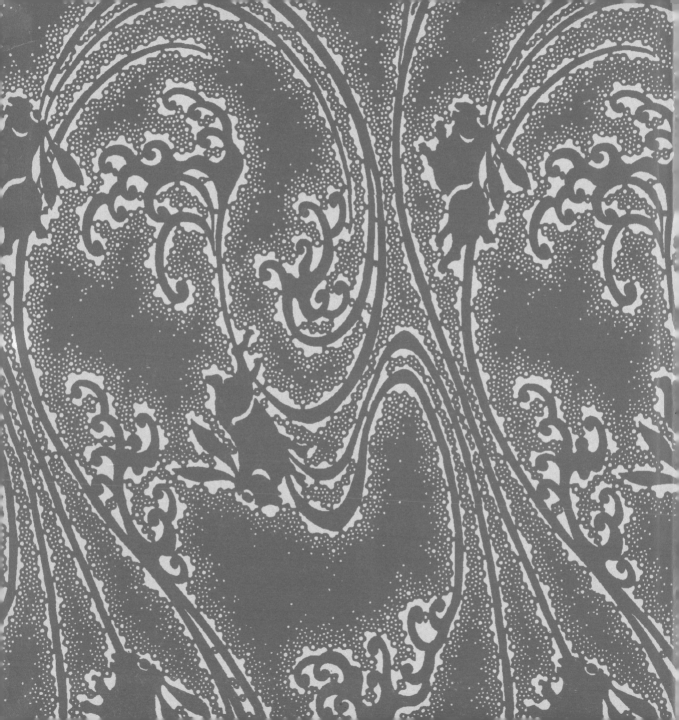